Joshua Seigal is a London-based poet leader. His children's books are publi Flying Eye, and he has performed a taken his poetry to the Edinburgh Fri Festival, the Cheltenham Literature Festival and the Bath Children's Literature Festival. Joshua is an official National Poetry Day Ambassador, and has held residencies at numerous schools. He is active on the spoken word poetry and comedy circuits.

www.joshuaseigal.co.uk

Advice to a Young Skydiver

Joshua Seigal

Burning Eye

Burning Eye Books
Never Knowingly
Mainstream

Copyright © 2018 Joshua Seigal

The author asserts the moral right under the Copyright, Designs and Patents Act 1988 to be identified as the author of this work.

All rights reserved. No part of this publication may be reproduced, stored in a retrieval system, or transmitted, in any form or by any means without the prior written consent of the author, nor be otherwise circulated in any form of binding or cover other than that in which it is published and without a similar condition being imposed on the subsequent purchaser.

This edition published by Burning Eye Books 2018

www.burningeye.co.uk

@burningeyebooks

Burning Eye Books
15 West Hill, Portishead, BS20 6LG

ISBN 978-1-911570-25-7

Advice to a Young Skydiver

CONTENTS

The First Thing You Should Know	8
Poet by Day, Accountant by Night	10
I'm So Clever	12
Flatmate	13
OCD	14
A Poem Commissioned for the 2015 British Biscuit Festival	15
Maplin Man	16
Lionel Urinal (& Friends)	18
Arbitree	20
At the Rockefeller Centre, New York	21
A Conversation	22
Jar-Gone	23
Out of the Minds of Babes	24
Leo	25
The Dad	26
A Fire Inside	27
In Year Two	28
'If' for Teachers	29
Writing on the Wall	30
Typical	31
Disappointing Fruit	32
Hate Is	33
Melancholy	34
Space Invader	36
Interlude	38
Manimal (A Children's Poem)	39
Barkin' Dog Blues	40
World Cup Slob	42
The Bouncer	44

An Epidemiologist's CV	45
An Agony Aunt's Calling Card	46
Hospital	47
David	48
If Only People	49
The Both of Us	50
Instead	51
Morning	52
Love Poem	53
Lalibela	54
A Poetry Gig at Which My Parents Are the Only Audience Members	55
Branson's Brother	56
How Do I Be a Success Like You?	57
Advice to a Young Skydiver	59

THE FIRST THING YOU SHOULD KNOW

is that this poem won't save you.
You won't find what you're looking for
among its little symbols.

You should know that this poem
was written on a manky notepad
with a half-empty biro. You can't
stuff your soul with paper;
you can't void the void with a pen.

You are falling. This poem is just
something to read on the way down.
This poem won't save you.
That's the first thing you should know.

The second thing you should know is

POET BY DAY, ACCOUNTANT BY NIGHT

I wake up in a bumble
as I tumble out of bed,
then I mumble as I fumble
with the jumble in my head.
I get myself all decked out
in my finest dressing gown,
count the seconds till I check out
and step out and on the town.

I can't wait to chuck the toady odes
and feel myself take flight,
'cause I'm a poet by day –
accountant by night.

I work the nine-to-fives,
finding ballads really cumbersome.
I really come alive
when I can get all hot and numbersome.
'Cause every working day
I'm bustin' stanzas to the maximum,
I'll axe the work for play,
put on my slacks and do a tax return.

I love to hit the office
and party till it's light,
'cause I'm a poet by day –
accountant by night.

Some people call me 'sell-out'
with my super-sonnet skills,
but I really want to yell out,
'I JUST RHYME TO PAY MY BILLS!'
And at dusk I step out brusquely
and assume a new identity.
I hang out in my suit
and be an absolute nonentity.

I pack away my Byron
and I change my name to… Dwight,
'cause I'm a poet by day –
accountant by night.

But now I'm thinking that the drinking
in the morning's getting dull,
and it may be wishful thinking
but it's clinking in my skull:
yes, I'm pining for the time
when I can ditch the wretched rhyme.
I've an itch to switch my pitch
and hit the finances full-time.

Yes, the figures give me vigour
as they trigger and ignite
and make blatant all the latent force
that gives my life some bite.
But for now I'll nurse my verses
as I curse the need to write,
'cause I'm a poet by day –
accountant by night.

Yeah, I'm a poet by day –
accountant by night.

I'M SO CLEVER

The layout of
this poem,   as you see, is not
quite right. The rhythm may
be perfect and
the rhyming might be tight, but
the formatting is   wonky which
will give
you quite a fright, and perpetuate
the viewpoint
that all poetry is

               shite.

FLATMATE

I'm staying in the flat
of my sister's friend.
To forestall stilted conversation
on the trip to the bathroom
I clean my teeth in my room,
spitting white gobs of toothpaste
into an empty pint glass
and leaving it on the desk.
I forget about it, until
my sister's friend walks in.
My stomach leaps into my mouth
at the thought that she may
have seen the cup.
I rush to assure her
that it isn't
what she thinks it is.
This doesn't make it
any less awkward.

OCD

Oh, CD!
Oh, CD!
I need to arrange you
alphabetically.

A POEM COMMISSIONED FOR THE 2015 BRITISH BISCUIT FESTIVAL

I like my bread short,
and my poems shorter.

MAPLIN MAN

In a world of commotions, emotions and feelings,
and other such jokes that can leave a bloke reeling,
a chap likes to hope for some comfort and healing –
a space to relax and unwind.

A place to be safe from life's ripples and eddies,
a place that is faithful and constant and steady,
a place where the pace isn't hectic or heady –
a place where you know what you'll find…

SO COME TO MAPLIN!
Come sup at our table!
You know where you are with a USB cable!
A lithium battery won't ever leave you!
A socket adapter won't cheat or deceive you!

YES, COME TO MAPLIN!
Rejoice in our manor!
Forget your divorce with a printer and scanner!
Your daughter's gone missing? Well, over you trundle –
come blow all your woes on our motherboard bundle.

In here there's no tricksters or Machiavellis,
just PC components and oversized tellies,
and dual format soundbars, yes, come fill your wellies
and pray at our altar of light.

Our trained Maplin chaplains, they know how to guide you.
So you have been let down and you have been lied to?
A broadband extender flex will not deride you –
in Maplin your future is bright.

YES, COME TO MAPLIN!
Be part of our union!
Kneel down in the pew of electric communion!
Your dad's had a stroke and your mum broke her hip?
Throw pain down the drain with an LED strip.

OH, COME TO MAPLIN!
Be king of the castle!
Come dress all your stress in predictable parcels.
Come flatten your feelings with MP3 players
at your best-loved high street electrics purveyors.

At Maplin you're cushty, you're cuddled, you're cared for,
so come get some hand tools and fill up your man drawer.
With Vodafone dongles you won't have a tiff.
A Behringer microphone's never not stiff.

At Maplin you're safe now, the world's in a lull.
A monitor won't call you 'nerdy' or 'dull'.
A portable speaker won't steal your wife.
So come down to Maplin
and feast
on your life.

LIONEL URINAL (& FRIENDS)

He lurks by the bar,
He's downing his beer,
He's lairy, he's sweary,
He's had two or three.
He chats up the birds.
There's nothing to fear
Until... he needs a wee.

For nothing panics good old Lionel
Like standing at the men's urinal.
It makes him sweat, it scares him rigid,
Catching sight of another man's digit.
Eyes straight ahead! Just keep on pishing!
Block out the view from your peripheral vision!
Gawk at the pork? No bloody way!
If you clock a cock you *must* be gay!

He's dancing away,
He's busting the moves,
He's healthy, he's wealthy,
He's flashing the cash.
He's loving the party vibe,
Loving the grooves
Until... he needs a slash.

For nothing tortures Micky McGee
Like a trip to the gentleman's WC.
He'll go to great lengths, he's determined, he's hell-bent
On avoiding the sight of another bloke's bell-end.
He'll don some blinkers, there's a lot at stake –
He might catch a glimpse of a trouser snake!
It's driving him nuts! He needs to get sectioned!
Penises flying in all directions!

He's pumping some iron,
He's lifting some weights,
He's hurly, he's burly,
He's fit as a fiddle.
He's flexing his biceps,
He's feeling just great
Until… he needs a widdle.

For nothing troubles our man Gareth
Like copping sight of some dude's phallus.
He gets palpitations, he breaks out in hives –
Eyes to the front! Don't look to the sides!
No other horror can compete
With an inadvertent peek of meat.

You'll be OK, mate. You'll struggle through.
But… is the guy next to you glancing at *you*??

ARBITREE

Elm.

AT THE ROCKEFELLER CENTRE, NEW YORK

We queued
to join the queue
to join the queue
to join the queue
to get in.

When we got in
we couldn't see anything
because of all the people.

So we queued
to join the queue
to join the queue
to join the queue
to get out.

The whole thing cost us
ninety dollars.

Somewhere
beyond the skyline
Rockefeller torched a cigar
and laughed.

A CONVERSATION

'Where are you from?'
'London.'
'No, I mean where are you FROM?'
'London.'
'No, I mean where are you REALLY from?'
'London.'
'No, I mean where are you from ORIGINALLY?'
'From my parents.'
'OK, so where are your PARENTS from?'
'Well, my mum grew up in Wales.'
'That's not what I mean.'
'Well, what do you mean, then?'
'Er… er… I mean why is your skin that colour?'

JAR-GONE

The screw-threaded
CT-finished
hermetically sealed
soda-lime glass receptacle
wherein the confit
of seed-bearing
angiospermic structures
was contained
has been irrevocably
mislaid.

OUT OF THE MINDS OF BABES

Children think some funny things,
it can really make you laugh:
I used to think that ethnic cleansing
referred to a foreigner in a bath.
I used to think that guerrilla warfare
meant monkeys fighting in the zoo,
and when my mum bought me a kit for gym
I said to Jim, 'It's for me, not for you.'
Yes, children think some funny things,
it can really make you titter:
I thought my cats were very tidy
since they had a box to put their litter.
I used to think a pharmacy
was where animals go when they're sick
and that the penalty box was a box to put pennies
when you got a penalty kick.
I used to think a 'concentration camp'
was a summer camp that was cruel,
where they made you concentrate really hard,
a bit like being at school.
But I knew where babies came from,
I didn't fall for the stork, unlike some –
since I ventured into my parents' room

and saw my dad fucking my mum.

LEO

is locked in the kitchen.
I'm outside with my mum and my sister.
My mum is panicking –

Turn the key, Leo. No, not that way, the other way.
Leo can barely reach anyway.
He doesn't understand.

Inside the kitchen our dinner is boiling over;
we can hear its hiss as the froth hits the flame.
Me and Danielle are giggling,

but Mum doesn't think it's funny –
Jesus Christ, you two, he's locked in there.
So Mum grabs a brick lying loose on the lawn,

smashes the panel on the kitchen door,
then reaches in to unlock it.
Later on she's on the phone to my dad,

telling him what happened.
As she's talking her words give way
to a trickle of tears.

I sit at the table, staring hard at my dinner.
I can't imagine eating ever again.
Leo sits in his high chair,   laughing.

THE DAD

is on the platform.
His baby son
is gurgling away
in the pushchair.
'Where's the train?'
asks the dad.
The boy says nothing.
'Point at the train for Daddy,'
says the dad.
Still the boy says nothing.
'Go on, point at the train for Daddy,'
says the dad.
The boy looks at his mum
but does not point
at the train.
The boy doesn't care
about the train
or about his dad.
'Point at the train
or we're not getting on,'
says the dad.
The dad looks over
at the mum.
He is angry, frustrated.
The boy has let him down.
The boy who won't
point at the train.

A FIRE INSIDE

Out in the garden, my dad gathers
the struts of wood that have been lying
behind the shed since last October.

He arranges them like a tepee
in the metal basket, then puts
scrunched-up newspaper underneath.

He lights one corner of the paper,
then the other, and I watch the fire
grow in the womb of the pile,

gathering strength as it feeds on old news
until finally it emerges, lapping the wood
like a hungry dog as my dad and I

stand back. The winter air
turns our breath to smoke.
'I've always loved fire,' he says.

IN YEAR TWO

she asked why twenty
wasn't called 'tenteen' instead.
'It just isn't,' the teacher said.

In Year Two she claimed, in Show and Tell,
that over the weekend she counted
up to 100, twice.

When asked in Year Two if anyone knew
how to spell 'of', and I piped up, 'O V,'
she replied straight away

with an 'O' and an 'F'
gently but firmly,
under her breath.

In Year Two I told the class
that I wanted to be an archaeologist.
I didn't know what that was. She did.

I didn't like her.

'IF' FOR TEACHERS

If you can keep your voice when all about you
Are using theirs to bellow over you;
If you can dish out rules when all kids flout you
But see the humour in their flouting too;
If you can care and not get tired of caring
Or, being dissed, maintain a steady poise,
Or, being sworn at, not give way to swearing,
And see the stillness in amongst the noise;

If you can plan but not make plans your mistress;
If you can chill and have a nice weekend;
If you can still take care of all your business
And not let children drive you round the bend;
If you can bear to see the gifts you've given
Received by ingrates with a sullen grunt,
Or feel the fuel diminish, but stay driven
And smile when the Head is being a... difficult person to work with;

If you can make an ally of a parent
And both look out for what you think is best
For Little Johnny when he has been errant
And hasn't done his work or passed his test;
If you can force your brain and heart and sinew
To teach the things that Ofsted says you should,
And so make sure the governors don't bin you
And that the school maintains its place as 'Good';

If you can talk with yobs and keep composure
Or plug away when they don't give a damn;
If you can act when there's been 'a disclosure'
And *not* display the news on Instagram;
If you can keep calm while you have to wing it
With sixty minutes' worth of 'drama games',
Yours is the class and everything that's in it,
And – which is more – you might not go insane.

WRITING ON THE WALL

It started off with doodles in places nobody could see – the room was due to be redecorated, and Mum said we could draw on the walls. Then entered the cocks and balls as the first wave of interlopers moved in. Every day I'd return from school to find my brother's friends. 'Call here for sex,' read one of their scrawls, followed by a classmate's name and number. Next there were pictures of each other's mothers *in flagrante* with various items of livestock. It's a wonder my parents stood for it as long as they did, come to think of it. The renovation happened later than had been expected. In the meantime I'd given in, daubed the walls with Tom Waits lyrics, and as I lay there on my back, feeling myself groped by the cartoon hands of adulthood, I considered calling that number.

TYPICAL

I bought a tin of
Alphabetti Spaghetti.
There were only O's.

DISAPPOINTING FRUIT

I had a shite apple
in Whitechapel.

HATE IS

after Adrian Henri

Hate is a pair of rusty old cans
Hate is a fan club without any fans
Hate is a papercut on the glans
Hate is

Hate is a bloody nose after a fight
Hate is a bus driver on Friday night
Hate is the toilet pan after a shite
Hate is

Hate is a puddle without any mops
Hate is a mugging without any cops
Hate is Jimmy Savile on *Top of the Pops*
Hate is

Hate is a polar without any bear
Hate is a drum kit without any snare
Hate is a massage from Tony Blair
Hate is

Hate is you and hate is me
Hate is shit rhyming, one two three
Hate is Joshua Seigal doing poetry
Hate is…

MELANCHOLY

Melancholy
Black bile
Rumpled trousers
Forced smile
Out of bed
Take the pills
Leave the packet
On the sill
Try to talk
No words left
Try to listen
Bored and deaf
In the car
Therapist
Talk things over
Make a list
Melancholy
Black hound
Insides trembling
Trouble-bound
Ditch your girl
It's over now
She fucks your best mate
What a cow
Read a book
Can't take it in
Can't concentrate
Above the din
Party next door
Don't want to go
A bunch of people
You won't know
Your ex is there
She says hello
She's with a guy
Get up and go
Chest contorted

Have a drink
Go outside
And have a think
Go back home
Start to cry
Remembering
That last goodbye
Rumpled trousers
Forced smile
Melancholy
Black bile.

SPACE INVADER

He's a space invader
A proxemical raider
Better drop him quickly like a hot potater

A whole bus free and he sits next to you
You can feel his breath as you stand in a queue
You're flecked with spittle whenever he speaks
You feel a little brittle as your patience creaks

He's a space attacker
A territory hacker
Better smack him swiftly in the knackers

He's the sleazy geezer with the drunken squeeze
You're on the train and he's touching your knees
He makes you sick with his icky shtick
Hanging with this wang is no picnic

He's a space intruder
A nuisance-exuder
He's the guy from accounts by the water cooler

You're chatting at a party and he's getting farty
He corners you in boredom with his 'arty' repartee
Regaling you with tales of the book that he's writing
You're giving him a look like you want to bite him

He's a lurking monstrosity
Run with velocity
His nose is too close to your physiognomy

You're on the tube and he's eyeing your *Metro*
He's more of a prick than a thorny hedgerow
He's all in your face, he's a graceless case
As he pitches a flag in your personal space

He's a space assailant
A nasty ailment
He's the Lionel Messi of social derailment

He's the bloke on coke with the shitty joke
And less charisma than an artichoke
He's like Ebola at an orgy
He'll chase you away like Georgie Porgie

He's an etiquette evader
A fun-blockader
Better watch out
He's a SPACE INVADER!

INTERLUDE

There was a young lady from Leicester,
who loved to annoy, vex and peicester.
She went down to Bicester.
I can't say I micester.
I hate her. In fact I deteicester.

MANIMAL (A CHILDREN'S POEM)

My dad is a **MANIMAL**.
In the morning he **WOLFS** down his breakfast.
I try to **MONKEY** around with him
but he says he can't **BEAR** it.
Sometimes he even goes **APE**
and tells me to stop **RABBITING** on
and **BADGERING** him.
Then he **BATS** me away
and **SWANS** off to work,
where he **TOADIES** around
and **FISHES** for money.
In the evening he **PIGS** out
and watches the **CRICKET**.

(optional adult ending)
Then he goes **DOGGING**.

BARKIN' DOG BLUES

Well, I let him in the garden
and he barks the whole night through,
yeah, I let him in the garden
and he barks the whole night through
and I can't get him in, baby,
and I don't know what to do.

I got the barkin' dog blues,
I got the barkin' dog blues
and now I got to go
and put on my barkin' dog shoes
to go and get him from the garden, baby,
yeah, I got the barkin' dog blues.

Well, I try to go to sleep, honey,
and he's scratchin' at my door,
yeah, I try to go to sleep, my lord,
and he's a-scratchin' at that door
and I dunno what he wants, baby –
what the hell he scratchin' for?
I got the barkin' dog blues.
I got the barkin' dog blues.
I'm tryin' to watch TV,
yeah, I'm tryin' to watch the news
but I can't hear a bloody word they sayin'.
I got the barkin' dog blues.

Well, I try to have a bath, baby,
and he's yappin' on the floor,
yeah, I try to have a bath, my lord,
and he's a-yappin' on that floor
and then he goes and jumps in with me, baby –
what the hell he do that for?

I got the barkin' dog blues,
I got the barkin' dog blues,
and I can't have a bath, baby,
or even go to the loo
without that damn dog barkin', baby –
what the hell am I gonna do?
I got the barkin' dog blues.

WORLD CUP SLOB

I'm a World Cup slob,
it's my full-time job
for a week every couple of years.
I belch and I scratch
and I watch every match
in my underwear, gulping my beer.

I'm driven to mania
watching Albania
play against Uzbekistan.
I tune in at two
for France v. Peru.
I'm Nigeria's number one fan.

I stare at the telly
whilst stuffing my belly
with doughnuts and pizza and chips.
When Switzerland score
I let out a roar
and when Uruguay lose I'm in bits.

The baby's unfed
and the hamster is dead.
I don't care; I am watching Ukraine.
I'd rather see China
than my wife's vagina.
'Not now, love, it's Holland v. Spain.'

My face is unshaved
as I sit in my cave
and converse in a series of grunts.
I watch with slack jaw
and when En-ger-land score
I spill Kettle Chips all down my front.

I'm a World Cup slob,
it's my full-time job
as I watch with my microwave dinner.
I'm fat and obscene,
I'm a slave to the screen,
in the Comatose Cup I'm the winner.

THE BOUNCER

He's a big fat fecker,
He's a right baboon
With fewer brain cells
Than a spoon.
He's thicker than an iron girder.
One GCSE: Attempted Murder.

He's a big fat fecker,
An orangutan.
For jaw dislocation
He's your man.
Hoodies and trainers? Ain't comin' in.
Throat ripped out and in the bin.

He's a big fat fecker,
A latter-day Bronson.
Massive biceps,
Tiny Johnson.
The Rudolf Hess of nightclub doorways,
He'll knock you out and send you floorways.

He's a big fat fecker
With a gleaming bonce.
'What you want,
You fecking ponce?'
Stanley knife; face cut to ribbons.
Less IQ points than a gibbon.

He's a big fat fecker,
Here he comes!
Footsteps
Like the thud of drums.

'Oi, oi! What's this that I can see?
Some posh boy writing poetry…?!'

AN EPIDEMIOLOGIST'S CV

Portfolio:
fought polio.

AN AGONY AUNT'S CALLING CARD

Dilemma?
Dial Emma.

HOSPITAL

Right, what
about this?
That lamppost
over there,
the one
about fifty
metres away,
the third
one along,
next to
the blue
Toyota – if
she hasn't
called by
the time
I reach it,
the news
will be
bad. Yes,
that's right.
And in
any case,
I'll walk
slowly. I'll
walk really,
really slowly.

DAVID

I never knew him. He died
of lung cancer before I was born.
He was an alcoholic too.
He passed all the exams
at medical school, but not
in the correct order, so he never
qualified as a doctor.
His wife never knew this.
He used to get up early
every morning, put on a suit,
say goodbye, and wander the streets
before going home at night.
Meanwhile his wife would sit inside,
unstitching the labels
on his Marks and Spencer jumpers
and sewing Harrods ones
in their place. She'd listen
for his key in the big oak door,
and when he returned,
without a word, they'd put
on a record and dance a dance,
the same one every night.

IF ONLY PEOPLE

spoke of the living
like they speak of the dead.

Just imagine:
we would go around declaring
how wonderful everyone is,
how kind they are,
how their hearts
(of gold)
are in the right place.

We would cherish urns
of dandruff and nail clippings,
forgive each other almost anything,
treat each bad word as sacrilege.
We would go out of our way
to attend the birthday parties
of distant relatives, declaiming it
'the right thing to do'.

Just think:
living itself would become an achievement.
The news would be a rolling dispatch
of everyone who made it through the day,

and when they died
we'd realise
that they weren't *that* great anyway.

THE BOTH OF US

I used to be a butterfly
but now I'm just a slug.
I used to be a toothy grin
but now I'm just a shrug.
I used to be a rainforest
but now I'm just a tree.
It used to be the both of us
but now it's only me.

I used to be an estuary
but now I'm just a brook.
I used to be a library
but now I'm just a book.
I used to be a sanctuary
but now I'm just a zoo.
It used to be the both of us
but now there isn't you.

I used to be a dinosaur
but now I'm just a mouse.
I used to be a cityscape
but now I'm just a house.
I used to be a bakery
but now I'm just a bun.
It used to be the both of us
but now there's only one.

I used to be a symphony
but now I'm just a note.
I used to be democracy
but now I'm just a vote.
I used to be Mount Everest
but now I'm just a stone.
It used to be the both of us
but now I'm all alone.

INSTEAD

There's a girl sitting across from me
        as the train approaches
                King's Cross at midnight.
      Having ventured earlier
that I have in fact read
        the book that lies undisturbed
                on her floral-dressed knee,
     I have been periodically conscious
throughout the journey
      of what, I think, is a smile.
I should talk to her, of course. I know this.
        Only when she starts prodding
            at a brick
      of a phone, however,
does this feeling of 'should'
      become one of 'must'.
I still don't do it, of course.
Instead I elect
      to write a poem about it.
            I reach for my bag
      in the overhead tray but,
            rifling through its crevices,
cannot find a pen.
      I should ask her for one, of course.
I know this.
But instead I write this poem down
      on my own shit phone,
           and wonder if
      she's writing one about me
on hers.

MORNING

and just before
she leaves
she says
she loves me
more than anything else
in the world
and it sits
in my stomach
warming my bones
like coal-smoke
in a powercut.

LOVE POEM

You're my beauty, my darling,
My sparrow, my starling,
My osprey, my eagle,
My dove.
You're my parrot, my crow,
My budgie, you know
You're my pigeon, my kestrel,
My love.
You're my penguin, my kiwi,
You know that you please me,
And please don't think me a nerd
When I say you're an owl.
Yes, I think you're fowl.
You know you're a right classy bird.

LALIBELA

We have a seat by the window.
We don't need to talk.
We can look out instead onto
the grey North London street.
This place is ours.

They know us in here,
know that we need this spot.
As we shake the rain off our coats
and I wrestle with your giant suitcase
our table waits with its white cloth.

In here, it doesn't matter
that we are what we are.
In here we breathe.
In here we have the table, the view,
the silence. In here we have

each other.

A POETRY GIG AT WHICH MY PARENTS ARE THE ONLY AUDIENCE MEMBERS

I hear my name, make my way to the stage. Mum's claps sound like a smacked bottom; Dad has a look on his face like he's just been presented with a three-year-old's finger painting. They shuffle sideways in their plastic chairs and Dad sips lukewarm cappuccino from a Styrofoam cup. I introduce myself, explain that tonight's menu is a choice between cerebral and frivolous. Mum's shrug tells me she doesn't care for long words. The mic stand is too short. I twiddle the knob to adjust the height, undo my top button, loosen my tie, fumble in my pocket for my lines. I begin with a joke, something about people not caring about poetry because poetry doesn't care about people. 'Get on with the poetry!' Dad calls. Mum's face comes alive as I take off my jacket, displaying dark wet patches round my armpits. Dad grins as I crowbar my shoes off my feet. I hesitate as I loosen my fly. 'What's the matter?' Mum asks. 'We've seen it all before.' Clothes gather on the floor as the tech guy dims the lights. I clear my throat, puff out my chest and recite the entire sum total of every word I've ever written, every thought I've ever had: 'Mum, Dad, here I am. Here I stand.'

BRANSON'S BROTHER

Have you heard of Branson's brother?
He lives on an estate in Southgate, London,
owns no car nor hint of a career,
and scratches a living from a part-time job
in the grounds of a local school.
Branson's brother doesn't have a wife
and, whilst not quite a virgin, enjoys
no intimacy with any other living soul.
He lingers awhile reading books at night,
quoting Kafka to the kids
in the playground the next day,
and stops to tie his brown suede shoes
on the steps of the local kebab shop.
From the window opposite his bed he sees
pigeons in the morning trees.
Branson's brother considers these:
flight means nothing and everything to him.

HOW DO I BE A SUCCESS LIKE YOU?

Outside the classroom, the other day,
a little boy came up to me and, tugging
at the hem of my garment, asked:
How do I be a success like you?

And I didn't know what to say.
You see, I'd never thought of myself that way.
Because after private school and two degrees
society does not tend to see reading poetry
to kids as a natural progression.
And sometimes it feels like I'm not listening in the lesson;
like this isn't 'real work' or the kind of thing
a *man* should do.
My parents tell me that I'm better than that,
that this isn't a proper job,
that of course giving kids the joy of words
is no bad thing, but to leave it to someone else
and to go out there and *be* someone.
Wear a suit, son.
Commute, son.
Be what we expect of you, son.
And of course *we* read poems and books to you, son,
but this wasn't an end in itself –
at no point did we dream that one day
you'd be doing such a thing for anyone
other than your own kids.
What are you, a glorified bloody babysitter?

And so the bitter taste at the back of my throat
when the boy asked,
How do I be a success like you?
arose from not believing it to be true.
It arose from skulking in the shadows
of people my age on £50k a year,
of people my age with their own flats and cars,
and even of the bloke at the bar who,
upon being told that I work with children,

drunkenly snorts *paedophile*, as though that
could be the only explanation for a man
wanting to do such a thing.

It arose from having memorised
the lines of a play
in which I play no part.
But no: through that boy's eyes
I saw myself anew.
So to the boy who asked me,
How do I be a success like you?
I say this:
Believe that what you're doing is worthwhile.
Believe that anyone who doubts you is mistaken.
Tell yourself every day that you can be whatever you want to be.
Tell yourself that success is not just reading
from someone else's script,
but believing what you say
or, even better, writing the words yourself.
And know that what counts is not whether
you've spelt them correctly, or whether
they're in the right order,
but that they. Are. *Yours.*

Success does not come in manuals.
Success is not flat-pack furniture,
and – you know what?
Success certainly doesn't come from listening to poems
about what success is.
So, son, do it *your* way.
Don't listen to what I say.

ADVICE TO A YOUNG SKYDIVER

You can do it, son.
Take deep breaths, and remember:
the ground's the limit.